RUTHLESS RHYMES
for
HEARTLESS HOMES
and More
RUTHLESS RHYMES
for
HEARTLESS HOMES

RUTHLESS RHYMES
for
HEARTLESS HOMES

and More
RUTHLESS RHYMES
for
HEARTLESS HOMES

HARRY GRAHAM

DOVER PUBLICATIONS, INC.
NEW YORK

This new Dover edition, first published in 1961, is an unabridged republication of the following:

Ruthless Rhymes for Heartless Homes, first published by Edward Arnold in 1899.

More Ruthless Rhymes for Heartless Homes, first published by Edward Arnold in 1930.

This edition designed by Geoffrey K. Mawby

Library of Congress Catalog Card Number: *61-661 98*

Manufactured in the United States of America

Dover Publications, Inc.
180 Varick Street
New York 14, N. Y.

CONTENTS

* These verses are printed with the kind permission of their authors.

CONTENTS

BEFORE

RUTHLESS RHYMES

OR HEARTLESS HOMES

Words by Col. D. Streamer

Illustrations by G.H.

With the most profound respect,
   I inscribe my dedication,
Realising its effect
   On this volume's circulation;
Since your name can hardly fail
To command a ready sale.

If the sunshine of your smile
   Lights our work, nor wanders off it,
Self and artist in a while
   Hope to share a handsome profit;
But, if you (and Fate) are cross,
Mr. Arnold bears the loss.

Do, I beg you, realise
   Your responsible position,
If this book should ever rise
   To a third or fourth edition;
Understand what you have done
If it fails to weather one!

THE STERN PARENT

Father heard his Children scream,
So he threw them in the stream,
Saying, as he drowned the third,
"Children should be seen, *not* heard!"

NURSE'S MISTAKE

Nurse, who peppered baby's face
  (She mistook it for a muffin),
Held her tongue and kept her place,
  "Laying low and sayin' nuffin' ";
Mother, seeing baby blinded,
Said, "Oh, nurse, how absent-minded!"

JIM; OR, THE DEFERRED LUNCHEON PARTY

When the line he tried to cross,
   The express ran into Jim;
Bitterly I mourn his loss —
   I was to have lunched with him.

THE FOND FATHER

Of Baby I was very fond,
   She'd won her father's heart;
So, when she fell into the pond,
   It gave me quite a start.

EQUANIMITY

Aunt Jane observed, the second time
    She tumbled off a bus,
"The step is short from the Sublime
    To the Ridiculous."

TENDER-HEARTEDNESS

Billy, in one of his nice new sashes,
Fell in the fire and was burnt to ashes;
Now, although the room grows chilly,
I haven't the heart to poke poor Billy.

UNSELFISHNESS

All those who see my children say,
"What sweet, what kind, what charming elves!"
They are so thoughtful, too, for they
Are *always* thinking of themselves.
It must be ages since I ceased
To wonder which I liked the least.

Such is their generosity,
That, when the roof began to fall,
They would not share the risk with me,
But said, "No, father, take it all!"
Yet I should love them more, I know,
If I did not dislike them so.

ECONOMY

My eldest son (his name is Jim)
   Came up to London and got lost;
I've had to advertise for him —
   You've no idea how much it cost.

And now, as it does not appear
   That I shall see my boy again,
I'm sad to think I've wasted near-
   -Ly £20, and all in vain!

APPRECIATION

Auntie, did you feel no pain
  Falling from that apple tree?
Will you do it, please, again?
  Cos my friend here didn't see.

OBSTRUCTION

You know "Lord's"? Well, once I played there,
   And a ball I hit to leg —
Struck the umpire's head and stayed there,
   As a nest retains an egg.
Hastily the wicket-keeper
   Seized a stump and prized about;

*   *   *

Had it gone two inches deeper
   He would ne'er have run me out.

*   *   *

This I minded all the more,
As my stroke was well worth four.

SELF-SACRIFICE

Father, chancing to chastise
  His indignant daughter Sue,
Said, "I hope you realise
  That this hurts me more than you."

Susan straightway ceased to roar;
  "If that's really true," said she,
"I can stand a good deal more;
  Pray go on, and don't mind me."

THE SHARK

Bob was bathing in the Bay,
When a Shark who passed that way
Punctured him in seven places;
— And he made *such* funny faces!

CARELESS JANE

Jane, who shot her Uncle Bill,
   Said his death did not affect her,
But, which makes it sadder still,
   Broke my "hammerless Ejector."

IMPETUOUS SAMUEL

Sam had spirits nought could check,
   And to-day, at breakfast, he
Broke his baby-sister's neck,
   So he shan't have jam for tea!

CALCULATING CLARA

O'er the rugged mountain's brow
    Clara threw the twins she nursed,
And remarked, "I wonder now
    Which will reach the bottom first?"

SCORCHING JOHN

John, who rode his Dunlop tyre
O'er the head of sweet Maria,

When she writhed in frightful pain,
Had to blow it out again.

PHILIP

Philip, foozling with his cleek,
Drove his ball through Helen's cheek;

Sad they bore her corpse away,
Seven up and six to play.

H. J. L. G.

MISFORTUNES NEVER COME SINGLY

Making toast at fireside,
Nurse fell in the grate and died;

And, what makes it ten times worse,
All the toast was burned *with* nurse.

THE PERILS OF OBESITY

Yesterday my gun exploded
When I thought it wasn't loaded;
Near my wife I pressed the trigger,
Chipped a fragment off her figure,

'Course I'm sorry, and all that,
But she shouldn't be so fat.

INCONSIDERATE HANNAH

Naughty little Hannah said
   She could make her Grandma whistle,
So, that night, inside her bed
   Placed some nettles and a thistle.

Though dear Grandma quite infirm is,
   Heartless Hannah watched her settle,
With her poor old epidermis
   Resting up against a nettle.

Suddenly she reached the thistle!
My! you should have heard her whistle!

       * * *

A successful plan was Hannah's,
But I cannot praise her manners.

MR. JONES

"There's been an accident!" they said,
"Your servant's cut in half; he's dead!"
"Indeed!" said Mr. Jones, "and please
Send me the half that's got my keys."

G. W.

LA COURSE INTERROMPUE

I.

Jean qui allait à Dijon
    (Il montait en bicyclette)
Rencontra un gros lion
    Qui se faisait la toilette.

LA COURSE INTERROMPUE

II.

Voilà Jean qui tombe à terre
Et le lion le digère!

* * *

Mon Dieu! Que c'est embêtant!
Il me devait quatre francs.

THE CHILDREN'S "DON'T"

I.

Don't tell Papa his nose is red
    As any rosebud or geranium,
Forbear to eye his hairless head
    Or criticise his cootlike cranium;
'Tis years of sorrow and of care
Have made his head come through his hair.

THE CHILDREN'S "DON'T"

II.

Don't give your endless guinea-pig
   (Wherein that animal may build a
Sufficient nest) the Sunday wig
   Of poor, dear, dull, deaf Aunt Matilda.
Oh, *don't* tie strings across her path,
Or empty beetles in her bath!

THE CHILDREN'S "DON'T"

III.

Don't ask your uncle why he's fat;
  Avoid upon his toe-joints treading;
Don't hide a hedgehog in his hat,
  Or bury brushes in his bedding.
He will not see the slightest sport
In pepper put into his port!

THE CHILDREN'S "DON'T"

IV.

Don't pull away the cherished chair
 On which Mamma intended sitting,
Nor yet prepare her session there
 By setting on the seat her knitting;
Pause ere you hurt her spine, I pray —
That is a game that *two* can play.

36

MORE
RUTHLESS RHYMES
for HEARTLESS HOMES

By

Harry Graham

Illustrated by

RIDGEWELL

LONDON: EDWARD ARNOLD & CO.

FOREWORD

Thirty years have passed since the English-speaking world was startled by the publication of a first volume of *Ruthless Rhymes for Heartless Homes.* In the opinion of my publisher, Mr. Edward Arnold, another shock of this nature is now due, and he has found means of persuading me to administer it. To recapture the first fine ruthless rapture is a difficult task; only the most vital considerations could have impelled me to attempt it.

I should like to take this opportunity of acknowledging my indebtedness to various sources of comfort and encouragement to which I have had recourse in the compilation of this work. My thanks are especially due to the Chancellor of the Exchequer, coupled with the names of the Commissioners of Inland Revenue, for the necessary stimulus; to Messrs. Fortnum and Mason, for their kind snow-boots and preserved ginger; to the Very Rev. the Dean of St. Paul's, for I forget exactly what; to Messrs. Spratt, for their admirable Puppy Biscuits; to Mr. Ridgewell, for his delightful illustrations; and to the Imperial Tobacco Company, for its constant and loving help. I am also grateful to Canon Gloy for his kindly promise to revise the Index, a promise which nothing but a pressing engagement to attend a Diocesan Synod could have prevented him from fulfilling.

Mr. Edward Arnold is most anxious that I should state that all the characters mentioned in these pages are entirely imaginary; no reference is made or intended to any living person. I am, indeed, very glad to hear this.

H. G.

39

INDIFFERENCE

When Grandmamma fell off the boat,
And couldn't swim (and wouldn't float),
Matilda just stood by and smiled.
I almost could have slapped the child.

PROVIDENCE

Fate moves in a mysterious way,
  As shown by Uncle Titus,
Who unexpectedly, one day,
  Was stricken with St. Vitus.
It proved a blessing in disguise,
  For, thanks to his condition,
He won the Non-Stop Dancing Prize
  At Wembley Exhibition.

TRAGEDY

That morning, when my wife eloped
With James, our chauffeur, how I moped!
What tragedies in life there are!
I'm dashed if I can start the car!

CONSOLATION

I sliced a brassey-shot at Rye,
And killed a luckless passer-by.
The ball rebounded off his head
And, landing on the green, lay dead.
His widow it must much console
To know 'twas thus I won the hole.

PRESENCE OF MIND

When, with my little daughter Blanche,
  I climbed the Alps, last summer,
I saw a dreadful avalanche
  About to overcome her;
And, as it swept her down the slope,
  I vaguely wondered whether
I should be wise to cut the rope
  That held us twain together.

      *   *   *

I must confess I'm glad I did,
But still I miss the child — poor kid!

COMPENSATION

Weep not for little Léonie,
Abducted by a French *Marquis!*
Though loss of honour was a wrench,
Just think how it's improved her French!

DISCIPLINE

To Percival, my youngest son,
Who cut his sister's throat, for fun,
I said: "Now, Percy! Manners, please!
You really mustn't be a tease!
I shall refuse, another time,
To take you to the Pantomime!"

OBSTINACY

I warned poor Mary of her fate,
But she *would* wed a plumber's mate!
For hours the choir was forced to sing
While he went back to fetch the ring.

UPLIFT

It seems that with Eternal Youth
   Great-Grandmamma is gifted,
For though (to tell the honest truth)
   Her face has twice been "lifted,"
To-day she doesn't look to me
A minute more than ninety-three.

CARELESSNESS

A window-cleaner in our street
Who fell (five storeys) at my feet
Impaled himself on my umbrella.
I said: "Come, come, you careless fella!
If my umbrella had been shut
You might have landed on my nut!"

L'ENFANT GLACÉ

When Baby's cries grew hard to bear
I popped him in the Frigidaire.
I never would have done so if
I'd known that he'd be frozen stiff.
My wife said: "George, I'm so unhappé!
Our darling's now completely *frappé!*"

WINTER SPORTS

The ice upon our pond's so thin
That poor Mamma has fallen in!
We cannot reach her from the shore
Until the surface freezes more.
Ah me, my heart grows weary waiting —
Besides, I want to have some skating.

THOUGHTLESSNESS

I never shall forget my shame
To find my son had forged my name.
If he'd had any thought for others
He might at least have forged his mother's.

OPPORTUNITY

When Mrs. Gorm (Aunt Eloïse)
Was stung to death by savage bees,
Her husband (Prebendary Gorm)
Put on his veil, and took the swarm.
He's publishing a book, next May,
On "How to Make Bee-keeping Pay."

LORD GORBALS

Once, as old Lord Gorbals motored
 Round his moors near John o' Groats,
He collided with a goatherd
 And a herd of forty goats.
By the time his car got through
They were all defunct but two.

Roughly he addressed the goatherd:
 "Dash my whiskers and my corns!
Can't you teach your goats, you dotard,
 That they ought to sound their horns?
Look, my A.A. badge is bent!
I've a mind to raise your rent!"

LONDON CALLING

When rabies attacked my Uncle Daniel,
And he had fits of barking like a spaniel,
The B.B.C. relayed him (from all stations)
At *Children's Hour* in "farmyard imitations."

QUIET FUN

My son Augustus, in the street, one day,
  Was feeling quite exceptionally merry.
A stranger asked him: "Can you show me, pray,
  The quickest way to Brompton Cemetery?"
"The quickest way? You bet I can!" said Gus,
  And pushed the fellow underneath a bus.

* * *

Whatever people say about my son,
He does enjoy his little bit of fun.

THRIFT

Last week our Parlourmaid withdrew
   Her savings from the Bank,
And sailed away to far Peru.
   Next day, her vessel sank!
She perished in an upper bunk,
And thus her sinking-fund was sunk.

THE LAST STRAW

Oh, gloomy, gloomy was the day
When poor Aunt Bertha ran away!
But Uncle finds to-day more black:
Aunt Bertha's threatening to run back!

BULL'S-EYE

At rifle-practice on the sands at Deal,
I fired at what I took to be a seal.
When later on I learnt 'twas sister Florrie
And that I'd shot her, I was very sorry.
But still it gratified me just a trifle
To find myself so expert with a rifle,
For, with so large a target as my sister,
I should have been a duffer if I'd missed her.

GRANDPAPA

Grandpapa fell down a drain;
Couldn't scramble out again.
Now he's floating down the sewer
There's one grandpapa the fewer.

WASTE

Our governess—would you believe
It?—drowned herself on Christmas Eve!
This was a waste, as, any way,
It would have been a holiday.

BISHOP PROUT

In Burma, once, while Bishop Prout
  Was preaching on Predestination,
There came a sudden waterspout
  And drowned the congregation.
"O Heav'n!" he cried, "why can't you wait
Until they've handed round the plate?"

BLACK AND TAN

Sun-bathing on the beach at Dover,
My wife became dark brown all over.
Upon the esplanade a man
Mistook her for the Aga Khan.
While on the Pier (where jokes are cheap)
They call her "The Calcutta Sweep."

CANON GLOY

One morning, just as Canon Gloy
   Was starting gaily for the station,
The Doctor said: "Your eldest boy
   Must have another operation!"
"What!" cried the Canon. "Not again?
That's *twice* he's made me miss my train!"

PATIENCE

When ski-ing in the Engadine
My hat blew off down a ravine.
My son, who went to fetch it back,
Slipped through an icy glacier's crack
And then got permanently stuck.
It really was infernal luck:
My hat was practically new—
I loved my little Henry too—
And I may have to wait for years
Till either of them reappears.

INDEX TO MORE RUTHLESS RHYMES

HOW TO TELL THE BIRDS FROM THE FLOWERS
by Robert Williams Wood

The late Robert Williams Wood was one of America's foremost physicists, the winner of the Rumford Premium, and many other scientific distinctions. Like Lewis Carroll and Bertrand Russell, however, he had a second side, perhaps even a secondary personality. His intimate friends knew him as a humorist almost without equal.

"How to Tell the Birds from the Flowers" and its sequel "Animal Anatomies" were the only collections of Wood's humor that were ever printed in book form. They were immediately recognized as classics, and within fifteen years of their original publication, went through some 28 different editions. They started a style in humor, a new type of nonsense verse that was widely imitated (though not excelled), and have had repercussions even to this day in advertising art.

Professor Wood specialized in a combination of misleading drawings and ridiculous verse. As his contemporaries recognized, Wood punned as ingeniously as Lewis Carroll, and drew as delightfully as Lear—with the same mixture of casual deliberate crudeness and subtlety,—and was as farfetchedly nonsensical as anyone could be.

Some critics of humor claim that a central theme runs through Wood's thought, and that his humor, which has delighted and still delights thousands, really has a deeper level. They claim that he demonstrates very ingeniously that surface similarities are not really similarities in nature, and that a confusion of levels of experience lends itself to delightful nonsense. Be this as it may, Wood's verse lingers in the memory of generations, and his title has passed into a popular saying that almost everyone recognizes.

This is the largest collection of Wood's drawings and verses ever printed. It contains the complete text of the latest edition of "How to Tell the Birds from the Flowers," (including "Animal Anatomies") together with three complete illustrated poems and two sketches that appeared in earlier editions and had been omitted. A new introduction has been written for this book by Margaret Wood White.

106 illustrations. 64pp. 5⅜ x 8.   Paperbound **75¢**

MAX AND MORITZ
by Wilhelm Busch
translated by H. Arthur Klein, M. C. Klein, and others

Wilhelm Busch (1832-1908), endowed with an equipotent facility with sketch-pad and rhyming dictionary, created during his career some of the most arresting sketches and drollest verses the world has ever seen. Few men since his time have shown the same ability to match simple yet penetrating pictures with rollicking, quotable verse. In his native Germany he is still by all odds the best-loved creator of illustrated light verse.

As a pen-and-ink draftsman, he excels in the delineation of complex physical movements with accuracy and simplicity of line. As a versifier, he is a master of the terse, subtle understatement and the slapdash rhyme. (Many of his pithy aphorisms have long since become folk sayings among the Germans.) The variety of tone and subject matter is wide: Busch is by turn malevolent, jovial, sardonic, diabolical and even bloodthirsty as he castigates hypocrisy, stodginess, stupidity, egotism, drunkenness, and other human foibles.

This unique collection—together with its companion volume, "Hypocritical Helena" —brings together a wide selection of Busch's very best work, allowing an interesting view of the unfolding of Busch's technique. In addition to the title piece, it contains "Ker and Plunk: Two Dogs and Two Boys" (Plisch und Plum), "The Egghead and the Two Cut-ups of Corinth" (Diogenes und die bösen Buben von Korinth), "The Raven-robbin' Rascals" (Das Rabennest), "Deceitful Henry" (Der hinterlistige Heinrich), "The Boy and the Popgun" (Das Pusterohr), "Ice-Peter" (Der Eispeter), "The Boy and the Pipe" (Krischan mit der Piepe), "Firm Faith" (Fester Glauben), "The Two Ducks and the Frog" (Die beiden Enten und der Frosch), and "Cat and Mouse" (Katze und Maus).

The English translations are both ingenious and faithful; in most cases they are the first English translations ever made. Those who do not read German may be certain that the original has been translated into English with its spiciness and sense intact. Both the German and the English appear side by side, so that readers of German may savor Busch's own delightful rhymes, while those who are learning German will find it an enjoyable way to gain familiarity with the language.

New selection of humorous pieces by Wilhelm Busch. English translation of "Max und Moritz" by C. T. Brooks. English translation of "Das Pusterohr," "Der Eispeter," and "Krischan mit der Piepe" by A. L. Alger. All other new translations prepared for this edition by H. Arthur Klein and M. C. Klein. Afterword by H. A. Klein. x + 205pp. 5⅜ x 8½. T181 Paperbound **$1.00**

THE DEVIL'S DICTIONARY
by Ambrose Bierce

CONTEMPT, n. The feeling of a prudent man for an enemy who is too formidable safely to be opposed.

EGOIST, n. A person of low taste, more interested in himself than in me.

MAUSOLEUM, n. The final and funniest folly of the rich.

In 1913, at the age of 71, Ambrose Bierce left for Mexico "with a pretty definite purpose, which, however, is not at present disclosable." He was never heard from again. Thus vanished America's greatest satirist in the classic tradition.

Since his disappearance, Bierce has been "rediscovered" about a dozen times, and always with a sense of surprise that America could have produced such a man. But a second glance at his work always indicates that only America could have produced him. Writing in the tradition of Swift and Shaw, he nevertheless aims his barbs at the specifically American institutions of which he was so much a part, impartially, but not indiscriminately, puncturing the sacred pomposities and cherished absurdities of American politics, business, religion, literature, and arts. He is as much a part of the American humor tradition as Mark Twain, Will Rogers, or Fred Allen.

"The Devil's Dictionary" reveals him in all his irreverent and sardonic splendor, japing mercilessly at our follies and self-delusions with all the classical, epigrammatic perfection of language that was his hallmark. Hundreds of pointed definitions, maxims, apocryphal quotations, and satirical verses attest to the power of his delightful, incisive wit. Bierce will always remain the favorite of a small coterie of enthusiasts, and of writers and speakers whom he supplies with, as H. L. Mencken said, "some of the most gorgeous witticisms of the English language." But he deserves a wider audience. His is the sort of unhurried, thoughtful humor that lasts.

Over 1,000 separate entries in alphabetical order.   5⅜ x 8.

Paperbound $1.00

B39148

Graham, Harry, 1874-1936.
  Ruthless rhymes for heartless homes;
and, More ruthless rhymes for heartless
homes.   New York, Dover Publications [1961]
  69 p. illus. (Dover edition, T930)

  I. Title. II. Title: More ruthless
rhymes for heart   less homes.
2/10/64 L/Z